Boxes

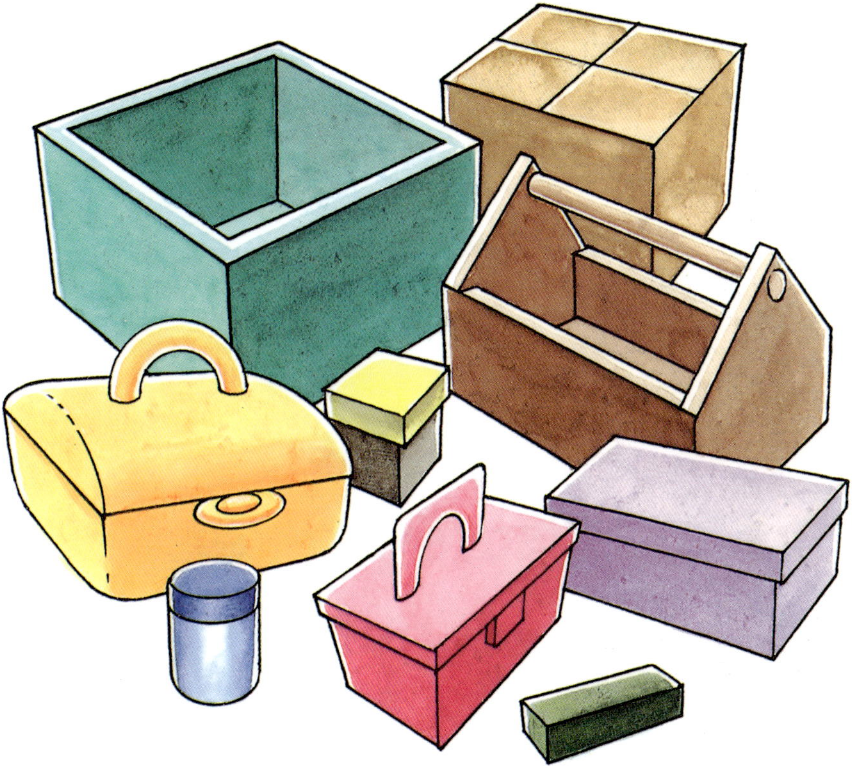

Written by Sandra Iversen
Illustrated by Clive Taylor

Find a box like this.

Put in a hammer.
Put in a screwdriver.
Put in a wrench.
Put in some nails.

You have a toolbox.

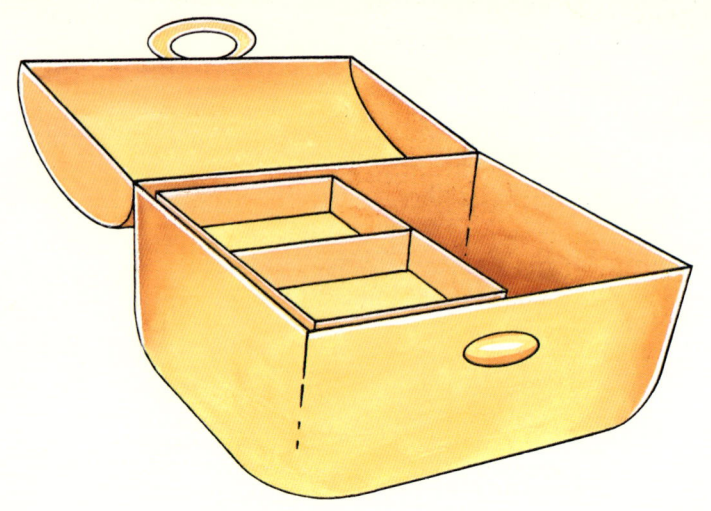

Find a box like this.

Put in some hooks.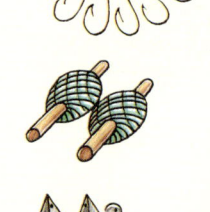
Put in some lines.
Put in some sinkers.
Put in some bait.

You have a fishing box.

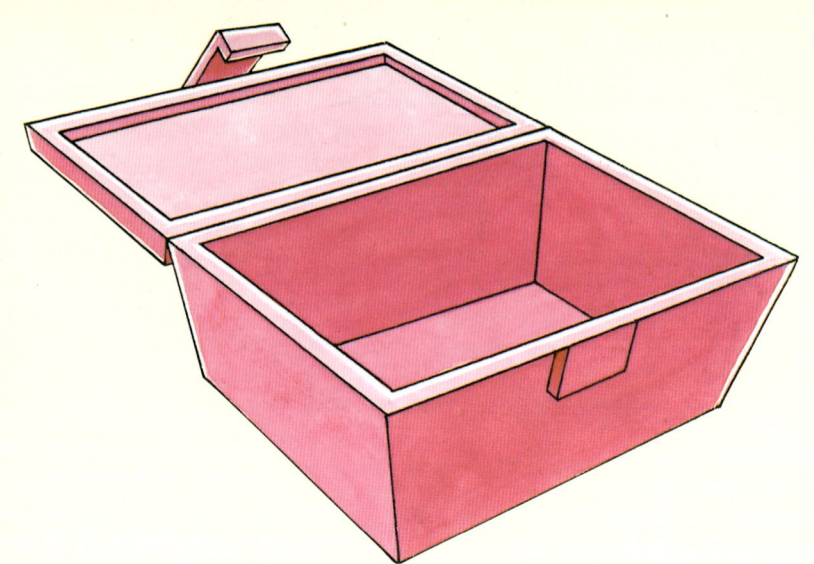

Find a box like this.

Put in an apple.
Put in a sandwich.
Put in a cookie.
Put in some juice.

You have a lunch box.

Find a box like this.

Put in some blocks.
Put in some games.
Put in some dolls.
Put in some books.

You have a toy box.